A LOOK AROUND SNAKES

by Janet Lambert
illustrated by Ray Keane

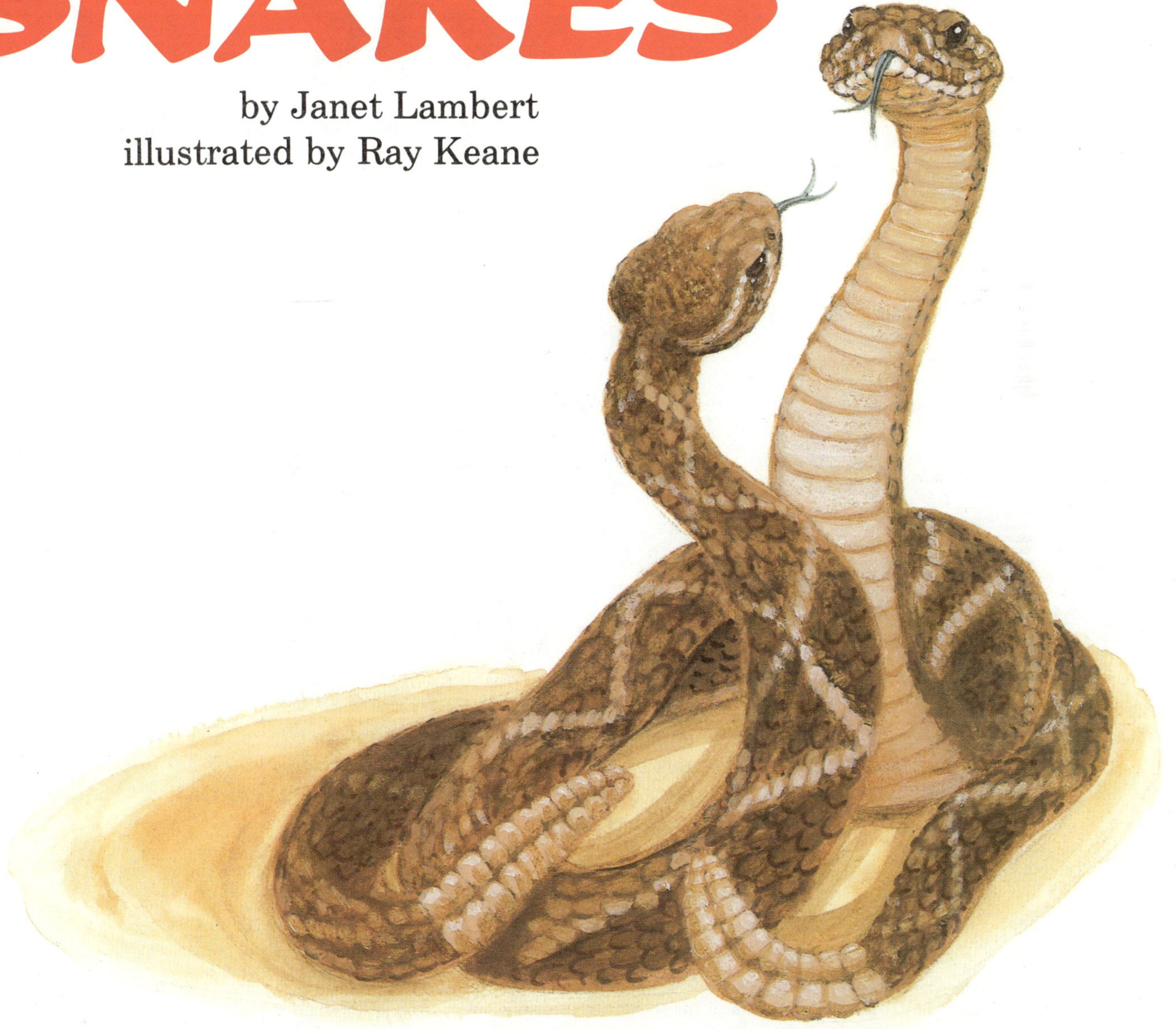

Special thanks to the Zoological Society of San Diego and to the Columbus Zoological Gardens; Columbus Zoo photographers Pat Asher, Dennis Roush, Nancy Staley, and Frank Postlewaite; and Columbus Zoo head keeper Dan Badgley and curator Mike Goode of the Reptiles and Amphibians Department.

Published by Willowisp Press, Inc.
401 E. Wilson Bridge Road, Worthington, Ohio 43085

Printed in the United States of America 10 9 8 7 6 5 4 ISBN 0-87406-258-6

Have you ever held a snake in your hands? You'll notice that a snake's skin is not wet and slimy at all. It is dry and smooth and covered with scales.

Snakes belong to the reptile family and are related to lizards. Unlike lizards, snakes do not have legs. Snakes also do not have eyelids. It isn't easy to tell when a snake is asleep. Snakes never close their eyes, not even to blink.

Snakes are cold-blooded. Unlike humans and other warm-blooded animals, they cannot live where temperatures are too hot or too cold. In the winter, some snakes tunnel underground where it is warmer. Other snakes hibernate in caves or dens until spring comes.

A snake's forked tongue is very sensitive. When the snake flicks its tongue in and out, it picks up scent particles from the air and ground. A snake can tell which animals are near from these scents.

Most snakes eat birds, insects, frogs, and small animals. Some snakes eat larger animals, and other snakes eat only eggs. All snakes swallow their food whole. An egg-eating snake uses special bones in its throat to break open the egg. The snake eats what's inside the egg and spits out the crushed shell.

Of the 2,700 kinds of snakes, about 400 are venomous. "Venomous" means that the snake's bite is poisonous. A venomous snake will bite its victim and release venom through holes in its fangs. The poison stuns or kills the prey quickly. Only venomous snakes have fangs.

The venomous pit viper has holes, or "pits," between its nose and eyes. These pit organs sense the body heat given off by warm-blooded animals. The pit viper can sense where its prey is hiding, even in the dark.

Vipers have distinct heart-shaped heads. Inside their heads are large venom glands where venom is stored.

Vipers have the longest fangs of all snakes. The fangs can grow to be two inches long. These movable fangs fold back against the roof of the viper's mouth when not being used.

Snakes will bite, or "strike," only when they must defend themselves. Snakes have many different ways of frightening their enemies. Snakes' enemies include people, some mammals, large birds, and even other snakes. King snakes will strike at an attacker. Venom from rattlesnakes does not affect king snakes.

The venomous African boomslang will try to hide in a tree if it is threatened. The color of its skin blends in with the branches.

If hiding doesn't work, the boomslang swells its neck to scare away its enemy. The snake looks bigger and more dangerous.

The rattlesnake is a type of pit viper with a special kind of tail. These poisonous snakes have a rattle at the end of their tails. The rattlesnake will shake its tail when threatened by an enemy.

The venomous horned viper and common sand viper make rattling noises, but they are not rattlesnakes. They coil themselves into balls. Then they rub together the rough scales on their sides to make a rattling sound.

The "horns" on the horned viper are really scales. These special scales help to protect the eyes and camouflage the head.

Nonvenomous constrictor snakes have a different way of protecting themselves. They coil their bodies around their prey and "constrict," or squeeze. When the victim stops breathing, the snake eats the animal's head first. Sometimes constrictors will kill animals as large as wild pigs or deer. Boas and pythons are constrictors.

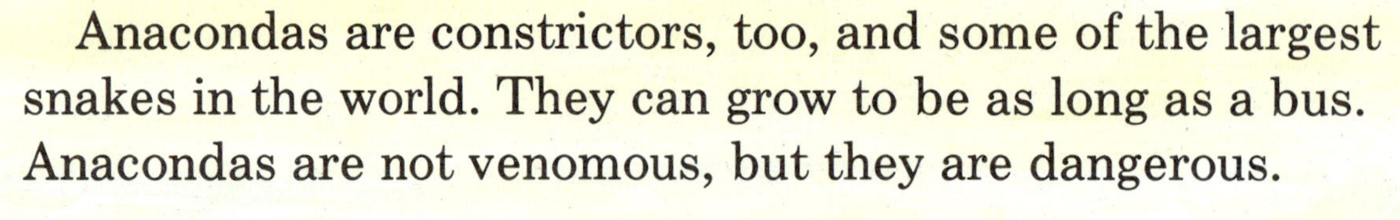

Anacondas are constrictors, too, and some of the largest snakes in the world. They can grow to be as long as a bus. Anacondas are not venomous, but they are dangerous.

Anacondas are water snakes and they live in swamps and slow-moving rivers of South America. These huge snakes usually stay near the edge of the water. They can swim and stay under water for more than ten minutes.

Some desert snakes can make themselves flat. They quickly cover themselves with sand when hiding from their enemies. The sidewinder rattlesnake does this to surprise its victims, too. Like other rattlesnakes, the sidewinder is a venomous pit viper.

The hognose snake is a very good actor. It will flip over on its back and play dead to avoid being attacked.

Many snakes have color patterns that are the same as their surroundings. These snakes blend in with the trees, rocks, desert, or plant life around them. Vine snakes are long, thin, green snakes. When the vine snake hangs motionless from a branch, its enemy cannot tell the snake from other vines.

Some harmless snakes look like their more dangerous cousins. These look-alike snakes are protected from birds and other enemies that might attack. The scarlet king snake looks like the deadly coral snake. Both snakes have red, black, and yellow markings.

Every few months, snakes shed their skin. Before a snake sheds, its old skin begins to look dull. Its eyes become cloudy-looking. A new skin is growing underneath.

The snake rubs its jaw against a rough piece of rock or wood. As the snake rubs, its muscles stretch. The old skin around its mouth breaks. The snake slowly slips off its old skin, inside out, usually in one piece. The snake's new skin is brightly colored and shiny.

Moving without legs is easy for a snake. A snake's muscles and the rough scales on its belly help the snake slither and climb. The scales are used like shovels. The scales "dig" into the ground or bark. Then, the muscles contract and pull the snake forward.

Some desert snakes move a different way, called "sidewinding." First, the snake uses its tail as an anchor. Then the snake arches its back and "throws" its head forward through the air. Its head lands in the sand first. The snake rolls the rest of its body sideways. Then it starts the motion again.

Cobras are some of the world's most poisonous snakes. When in danger, the cobra lifts its head and spreads its neck to look like a hood. Some cobras will spit venom into the eyes of their victims.

Cobras have been known to attack people and animals of all sizes, even elephants.

Many people consider cobras to be mysterious and full of magical powers. In India, crowds gather around a snake charmer as he plays his pipe. It looks like the cobra is "dancing." The snake is really following the motions of the snake charmer and his pipe.

Scientists "milk" snakes by pressing on the venom glands. The venom is then drained from the snake's fangs. Some medicines made from snake venom help stop bleeding and prevent blood from clotting. Venom mixed with other substances is used to treat snakebites. Researchers have experimented with using mixtures made from snake venom to fight cancer.

Since ancient times temple vipers have been considered good luck. People who believe this will not harm the vipers. They allow the vipers to live in trees near their homes. Temple vipers help keep away rodents and other pests.

Snakes make interesting pets. They are clean and quiet and don't require a lot of care. The biggest problem may be finding the right kind of food for your pet snake.

Before you get a pet snake, talk to a snake expert at the zoo or a pet store. Make sure you select a harmless snake. Some snakes, like the boa, might make good pets, but they grow to be very large. You must be sure your pet has enough room.

Remember these points when you go in a wilderness area.

- Wear leather high-top boots or shoes, and loose-fitting pants.
- Check for snakes before you reach or step into unseen places. Wear leather gloves when climbing.
- If you hear a rattling sound, move away slowly and quietly.
- Do not pick up a snake with your hands unless you are sure it is harmless.

If a snake bites you, take these important actions.

1. Try to get a good look at the snake.
2. Go to a doctor right away.
3. Stay calm and quiet. Do not move around.
4. Do not treat the bite yourself.

INDEX